SEX

SECRETS
OF SUCCESS

Art Director

John Clement

Series Editor

Alex Woodcock- Clarke

Printed and bound by Whitstable Litho, Millstrood Road,

Whitstable, Kent.

ISBN 1 899299 20 3

First published in Great Britain in 1994 by Golden Rule Publications, Eldon Lodge, 52 Victoria Road, London W8 5RQ.

Tel 071-937 3324. Fax 071-937 1137

THE FAIRER SEX

SECRETS OF SUCCESS

by

A B Crombie

SUCCESS WITH THE FAIRER SEX

Exactly which sex is the fairer has been a much debated point for many years.

Men are cute, there is no question of that, but women are cuter. That does not necessarily mean they are nicer. The Leopard Seal is one of the cutest, furriest, fluffiest creatures in the animal kingdom but try and stroke its trembly whiskers and it'll take off your hand somewhere at the armpit and use it as an ashtray.

For the purposes of this book, we shall assume that women are fairer than men. Why not give them a break? Women have to go through so many things that men can't even get their minds around (if we have to spell it out - periods, childbirth and menopause). And anyway, women are soft, sweet, gentle, lovely, wunnerful human beings - why do such

5

things happen to them?

Now there are men for whom success with the fairer sex is not an issue. They are innately successful. Their profiles are chiselled, their torsos gleam with healthy perspiration, their thighs are like tugboats, their hair is neither greasy nor damaged but gleams with the unnatural lustre only found in Gillette Sensor ads, they have the charisma of a Harley Street gynaecologist, the charm of a baby panda and the wisdom of an elderly jockey rounding Tattersal's Corner on the inside and their whip out of camera shot. This elite band of men total about 6 in the world, and this little guide is unnecessary to them. They are all of them Greek gods. The rest of you are the equivalent of god damned Greeks and for you this guide is essential.

It will tell you how to find the goddess of your dreams, woo her, enchant her, capture her and, if necessary, how to dispose of the body afterwards.. It will tell you the pitfalls with which you will be faced, the expectations you should have and the expectations she will have of you. Above all, it will give you the confidence to get out, get lucky, get laid and get lost and still leave a dazed, car-wreck survivor smile on the ruby lips of your lady.

Success takes commitment, not necessarily to the woman, but absolutely to the art. Remember that until you reach maturity (95?) There is no such thing as too many women or too much of a good thing.

THE ESSENTIALS

However great or wonderful a man thinks he is, he will be seen in a very different light by the woman of his dreams, his nightmares or any woman at all for that matter.

The macho image of a lad out with his mates swilling lager, or seeing how many weights he can lift before bedtime may do a great deal for the light that his mates see him in, but the only woman who will be impressed is the one who can either drink more than he can or can lift more than he can.

Deodorant

The first thing that any successful man needs to invest in, and success need not be very expensive, is a decent deodorant. What smells like muscle to a man smells like a skunk with Irritable Bowel Syndrome to a woman. Try any good chemist, late night supermarket, ordinary supermarket, paper shop or anywhere at all really. It doesn't matter which make it is as long as it works.

8

Butt

Next important item is a cute butt. If you haven't got one, work on it. It helps, we assure you. The first things women notice in a man are his eyes and his bottom. You can't do much about the eyes unless you are prepared to go through the discomfort of wearing coloured contact lenses, but you can do something about those buttocks. A little shoulder width doesn't hurt either. Come on, do you really think anyone really wants to be seen with the whimp from the "Mr. Muscle" ads? The only reason Hugh Grant gets all those chicks is that they can fit into everything in his wardrobe including, probably, his jockstrap.

A Woman

Probably the most important piece of equipment, though is a woman on your arm. It is true that there might be other things that look equally good on your arm like a gold Rolex or a falcon but women will be intrigued and not a little bit jealous to see one of their sisters clinging to your bicep like a vaccination mark. They will also feel excited that they are being wooed when the man in front of them obviously has no problem with women. For this you must have a little black book, and note down all your successes, which of course will be numerous when you have finished reading this book. For those of you whose little black book is filled, not with the names of devastating, sexy girls, but the engine numbers of trains or computer codes, then go out and get a woman at once. Mental nurses are tremendously understanding and clinging and, if they won't help, perhaps they might know a patient who might.

Too Many Women

The other problem you will find yourself faced with is a plethora of women. Go into any bar, restaurant, office, club, the Heston Services on the M4 for God's sake and you are surrounded by women.

They come in all shapes and sizes, and they speak a completely different language. (At least, the girls with whom you wish to be successful do, we assure you). What is more disturbing is that often they speak different dialects of woman speak. You might get to understand one, but you may well be completely flummoxed by the next. It is important to remember that a man who masters the art of woman speak is considered not only seriously disturbing to the female population, but seriously disturbed as well. So when you think you might be getting somewhere with their language, it is time to move on to the next sector.

Large Men

You will find on your route to success that there are always other men on the prowl around the woman of your choice. They will have tattoos that depict scenes of violence which would have taxed the imagination of Breughel. They will be bigger than you and nastier. Their muscles will bulge through their shell-suits like walnuts in a condom. They will have tiny eyes, enormous lantern jaws and low Planet-Of-The-Apes foreheads- in fact, the only thing uglier than these men will be their Rottweillers. Do not be intimidated. As the fabulous man you are, you will have good taste, and your selected lady will undoubtedly have more than one admirer.

Get rid of her unsightly companion by inviting him

"to come outside and settle this like a man". When you get outside, give him £100 or as much money as you have on you. If he argues that such a clearance sale cash offer offends his sensibilities, then brain him with a length of lead piping you have hidden up your sleeve. If, after a swift piping, he doesn't fall to the ground like a stoned crow but, instead, just stands there, shaking his head sadly, run away - and run away fast because if he catches you this Neanderthal will twist you into an unusual shape and use you as a trinket for his charm bracelet. No woman is worth it.

Sex

Women are fascinated by sex. What do think they talk about when you have a gaggle of them together? No, it is not the marital problems of Grant and Sharon from "Eastenders" and neither is it the shocking anti-female discrimination of the British Lions Rugby Team selectors. It is rumpy-pumpy that so exercises their minds.

Though you think that men are the only ones who talk about the bit of skirt they had last night, women will be going into great·detail about what sort of foreplay there was, how long it took, what shape the man's penis was and what size. If you have something to be worried about, better make love in the dark until you know each other better. Otherwise, your mutual acquaintances will look at you in a completely different light - and making the sign of the cross as they do so.

PROBLEMS TO AVOID

Women in groups

It is difficult to corner one woman out of a large party of women. Remember that you won't understand what on earth they are talking about, but if you make a move on any of them, you can be sure that you will become the main topic of conversation.

Besides, women together are not only bitchy, they have a tendency to egg each other on, whipping each other up into a fury. One minute they're a happy, chattering mob of young ladies - next thing you know, you're dealing with a lynching party straight out of "To Kill A Mocking Bird".

If there are men involved in the party, you may be OK, but on the other hand they may be rivals who have got there first.

Women on their own

She's either a sad wallflower, or she wants to be on her own. If she starts talking to you, you're safe, but if you start talking to her and she is just a little bit put out, the bar man will throw you out.

Offer her a drink, the paper, a comment on the weather. If it is accepted, with thanks and a smile, you may be lucky. If rejected, leave well alone.

Places Where It's Wrong To Approach a Woman On Her Own.

In the confessional box.

On the hard shoulder of any motorway.

When she's having a smear test.

Just outside the Inns of Court after a messy divorce and she realises she'll be paying alimony to a lazy, good-for-nothing toyboy for the rest of her livelong days.

When she's holed up in a MacDonalds with a sub-machine gun holding five kiddies hostage and demanding that Salman Rushdie be sent in to her alone.

15

Places Where It's All Right to Approach A Woman On Her Own.

Library/book shop.
Art galleries.
Pet shops.
The golf range.
The bus stop or train platform.
When she's just received a record pools cheque from Cilla Black.

And so to the rules of success.

FIRST
IMPRESSIONS

The things women look for are:

Credit Cards
Gold American Express card. Platinum is too flash, and Corporate just means you are spending someone else's money on them. Gold means that you have income over a certain limit. Girls needn't know that you have had it since your good years and that if it's actually ever used it will bounce

A Bulge
A decent sized bulge in the trousers. The following story will demonstrate its efficacy.

One of our friends was walking on the beach. A fair

enough physique, but nothing special. The girls didn't give him a second look. What was he doing wrong? A friend of his, who was more lucky in the love department, gave him a tip: "Shove a potato down your trunks and I swear the girls will come running. I'll come along and watch". Next day, our man got a large, firm potato, slipped it in his trunks and, while his friend observed from a discreet distance, sauntered along the beach. True enough, the girls did run - but screaming and in the opposite direction. He asked his friend what had gone wrong. "OK. That was very good for a first attempt. Now let's try putting the potato down the front of the trunks".

If nature has not been that generous, an old sock will do the trick. However, if you wear boxers, said sock has a tendency of falling out, so a neat bit of Sellotape should do the trick. If perchance you get lucky, and find yourself removing your underwear in close proximity to a member of the fairer sex, make sure you removed the sock beforehand - by that time it won't matter any longer.

The more expensive and permanent way is to have

plastic surgery. If this makes you cringe, just think what women go through with nose jobs and face lifts!

Good Manners

However tough nosed, feminist or hard-hatted, women still appreciate having doors opened for them, a polite greeting and still prefer the man to pick up the tab.

You may not think that this is fair - if they want equality, they should damn well pay for it - and in theory they would probably agree with you. But it doesn't work like that. Do not go too far though. There is no need to stand up when a lady goes to the loo. Modern women find this not only unnerving, they also find it rather patronising (though it's only because you've drawn attention to them and the fact that after one and a half gin-and-slimlines the pressure gauge on their bladder goes over into the red).

Generosity and Spontaneity .

However much a man tries to persuade himself and his friends that less is more, three dozen red roses will go down a whole heap better than a single stem. However, you must not let her get used to such gestures, because it can becomes an extremely expensive habit, and once it's a habit it's lost its usefulness. Yes, you could begin by coming up smelling of roses but, go too far and you'll just end up smelling of the stuff they're buried in.

Good Taste.

Whoever told you years ago that women like soft centres was talking about their grandmother who lost all her teeth as a sparring partner for Rocky Marciano in the 50's. Why should modern women, who are under a social compulsion to be as thin as clothes hangers, actually welcome your Large Promotional Size box of Cadbury's Milk Tray. This box with its decorative ribbon contains more calories than a bucketful of lard garnished with pork scratchings and, as such, is on the Proscribed List of the Cambridge Diet. The only way you'll get away with giving a woman a box of sickly sweet soft sugary muck is to scale a 20 foot building with them or to hang suspended from a helicopter at 700 foot above sea level.

Clean Finger Nails.

This is vitally important. If a woman is going to let your hands start roving, she wants to know where they've been. And with the engine oil spread thick under your nails with a whole load of other muck she will be in a state of major distress. You've got to look as though you have made some sort of an effort and not as if you've just withdrawn it from the backside of a cow during auditions for the Christopher Timothy part in "All Creatures Great And Small".

Sophistication

The hand crawling like a tarantula along the back of the cinema seat might have worked when you were 17, but it isn't going to work any longer. It invokes ridicule and pity, and besides it means that neither of you are able to concentrate on the film, which no doubt you paid good money (twice) to see. Where is your poise, your panache, your sophistication? Why try the full frontal assault when you can succeed with the oblique approach? Women like to be wooed by a man who is a cross between "Papa" from the Renault Clio ads and Douglas Hurd -

but don't go round practising saying "Ni-cole?" with an upturned Mr. Whippy ice-cream cone on your head too hard because the moment your wooing is successful, your woman will expect you to drop all pretence of urbanity and transform yourself into a sexually urgent rhinoceros. And they say men can't make up their minds.

The Female Orgasm

A woman will expect you to know what a female orgasm is and though not necessarily requiring it, she will want to be given the choice. A female orgasm is accompanied by hysterical screams, a wild convulsion and, more often that not, deep scratches across a man's body. Some unlucky men have never come across a female orgasm. We are not embarrassed to tell you what it is. A female orgasm is a large brown sewer rat (Latin name, "Rattus Norwegicus") and you should always keep one in a plain box beside your bed. Then, after three hours of sexual foreplay in which you have developed lock-jaw and worn your fingertips down to the first knuckle, and she is still complaining that "You still haven't given me an orgasm", you should hand her the box. Screams, convulsions and scratching will follow immediately. To achieve multiple orgasm, hide the rat in her tights and watch as your lady dresses in the morning.

A WOMAN'S TONGUE

Women speak a different language - the mother tongue. The following words are part of women's speak and though they are translated into English, this is confidential information and not to be mentioned in the company of women under any circumstance whatsoever. Women are extremely touchy on these subjects.

VPL

Visible Panty Line. Woman wearing panties that just don't fit so you can see the line of her knickers through her skirts or trousers

PMT/PMS

Pre-Menstrual Tension or Pre-Menstrual Stress. This is a depression that many women suffer from just before their period, and is considered the source of their major unpredictability. Suggesting that a woman suffers from this syndrome, particularly when it is true, is likely to get you a clip over the head with the back of a hand, or a clip round the back with the head of a machete. There are pills which a doctor will happily prescribe to combat the effects of PMT, but if a woman is rational enough to know that she needs them, then she doesn't.

Bodily Hair

Women spend hours, fortunes and large amounts of emotion on disposing of bodily hair. Those who don't are either genetically odd, have suffered some terrible disease, are proactive feminists, or are just not very good at being proud of themselves.

There are those who haven't this week, or have put it off for a while, but they meant to, honestly. You may not think it is very important, but it is as important to a woman as bald patches are to men.

Wrinkles.

This is death to mention. Women spend hours every week in front of the mirror, massaging useless creams into their faces to pre-empt or to dispose of wrinkles. A woman always wants to be a girl, and getting older is anathema to her. Wrinkles are the first sign of ageing. Along with sagging breasts (which you also mention at your peril).

Cellulite.

The female Polyfilla To be as polite as possible, this is the unsightly fat that accumulates on a woman's bottom and thighs as she gets older. Women call it the Orange Peel effect, but it is more,like the development of finger grips on her backside. Nothing distresses her more. If a woman ever asks you about cellulite, say you have never heard of it, or maybe ask her if it is the new type of mobile phone that you've been reading about.

Weight.

When a woman asks you if she's put on weight, you must never, ever tell her the truth. If she does ask, then she knows she has, but she is not demanding the truth, only a little understanding. It doesn't matter if she looks like a sea cow inflated by a bicycle pump, the answer is always: "No, no, not at all. Well, perhaps just a little. But I like you that way". Just don't let her get on top during the grateful sex afterwards - she'll crush you like an avalanche.

Make-Up.

This is what a woman adorns herself with to make herself (she thinks) even more attractive. Women think that men can't see that they're wearing any, and they assume that you believe that she looks like that naturally. This can be a little bit of a problem when she is wearing blue and gold eye-shadow, and scarlet lipstick, but try just saying that she looks nice! Do not say: "Gorblimey, you look like an explosion in a Special Effects Department".

DIFFERENT VARIETIES OF WOMEN

Women can be divided into types. They would not think this kind, but it is true. The basic division is between career and domestic, but most women on either side of the line hanker after something that the other has got. If they didn't they would be very dull indeed. Each sector of women has varying aims and goals in life, and has to be approached , seen and conquered differently.

THE CAREER WOMAN

The career woman has her own income, her own tastes and, most of all, she has a truly impressive ambition. Her ego walks through the door just in front of her, though they fight each other for pole position. Her labels are expensive. Her hair is done, and she wears her self control like body armour. She is one hell of a challenge to any man who decides to take her on. Any simple chat-up will make her feel challenged to give a firm but pure put down. But she has huge advantages too. She has her own friends and her own interests. She doesn't need "keeping" and it means that you can go down to the pub and watch the football with your mates

The Pushy Media Woman

Media women can be split into two categories. There is the right wing media woman. She's in advertising or PR. She may even write for the diaries. She's public school, with public school looks. Daddy does something important, or at any rate Daddy earns important money. She lives a life that plays up to her huge expense account and massive overdraft. She knows more famous people than you ever heard of (and that's the point). Her feet haven't touched the ground since she left university (which was Exeter, Bristol, Durham or Edinburgh). Because she's the girl who knows everybody, she'll always be out and about, with a smile that could be tattooed on her face. She's really looking for a husband because she is quite sure that God didn't put her on this earth to work very hard, and by the time she's 26 she will probably have achieved that.

The Whingeing Media Woman

Then there is the left wing media woman - She started on a journalism course and now writes for the Guardian, does publicity for Green Peace or runs the planning department of some huge advertising company. She doesn't go on diets - she ties herself to a bulldozer on Twyford Down and goes on hunger strike for four days. She may not be a public school girl, but she probably went to Oxford or Cambridge. She has a chip the size of a sweet potato on her shoulder and she's bound to be a feminist. By the time she's got to her 26th birthday she has realised that there is a reason she has gone this far in the business. Everyone else is so parochial! Then, if she has anything about her, she gets bored and looks for something else to do. She'll probably want to become a war correspondent like the media woman she so much admires.

There are not many media women over the age of 35. Pushy has left advertising to write 800 page sex and shopping blockbusters with single-word titles such as "Scruples" or "Diamonds" or "Studs" which reveal deep-seated wish fulfilment anxieties, because she doesn't have enough of any of them. The Whinger has also left the hard-nosed world of communications - she now works for Channel 4, probably as Assistant Coordinator of the Asian Woman's Oppression Department.

Where to meet her

You know that little cocktail party that you thinking of skipping? Don't. She'll be there, being charming to everyone, "Networking" the room, drinking slightly too much and gossiping with the other media girls in the ladies'. Get yourself introduced. There'll be someone in the room that knows her. You could just go up to her and strike up a conversation. But beware. Conversation is her strength, with her specialist subject being herself. Once you've got her going, you'll never stop her - you'll get it all, the brutal boyfriends, the lack of self-esteem, the pledge to invest her personal life in her career, her success in a world-dominated by men, her pledge to help others whatever the costs, the drinking problem bravely overcome, the business-plan she has created that will take her from Peckham to Mayfair... Don't bother listening - she's just working out the plot of her first novel or her first hard-hitting social documentary entitled, "Woman - Aren't You Glorious?"

Pushy

Loiter outside a reasonably expensive beauty parlour on a Saturday morning. Every week is just so exhilarating that she needs to recover so she looks her best for the weekend:

Harvey Nichols is the media girls Mecca. She buys her clothes there, shops for food there, drinks there, eats there and very possibly sleeps there. This is where her aspirations lie. Do not disturb her when she is hunting through the sales rails. She has got far more important things on her mind than mere men. Being the salesman won't help either - she'll think of you as just a servant. Much better to catch her in the food halls. Her defences are down. She's buying things she can't afford, and then she's going to eat them. She's likely to be on her own, because she doesn't want her companions to see how many calories she's going to consume, or in fact what ordinary things she really buys.

The Whinger

Find a suitably P.C. rally. Gay Rights will do, but she might have a rather strange perception of you. You'll probably be more comfortable at Friends of the Earth or Rights for Women. The surest way, of course, is to get yourself involved in some activist movement, get arrested whilst on video and then demand that you are interviewed by her. However, if you are convicted of whatever you have committed, you will have little chance of success from then on. Unless she chooses to leads your "Free The Hemel Hempstead One" campaign but then she'll probably get off with the Home Secretary.

What music to play

They'll both love the ballet and light classical music. Media 2 may well go for the heavier stuff too-especially the Ride of the Valkyrie, but perhaps it is not that suitable for a first date. Try Al Jarreau or a touch of Mozart.

What to wear.

Both Pushy and The Whinger will be attracted by the same type. They meet so many people that you will have quite a lot to live up to. A trendy leather jacket, whether Chevignon or Armani, will go down a treat. A touch of the unshaven and unkempt look will excite them. Do not try the well cut suit. This will remind them of a client or an interviewee, and they will treat you accordingly. The impression you want to give is of a photo-journalist, a maverick who breaks the rules but is always in great demand because he delivers results; one who has just come back from some third-world sink-spot where "he has just seen too much". Give the impression that behind your 1000-yard-stare is a sensitive, yearning spirit that you hide behind a brusque nonchalance. You will probably appear as "André" or "Buck" in chapter 4 of the novel.

Where to take her.

Well she's been to a lot of places, either on her expenses or on somebody else's. She is the woman who is professionally wined and dined. She's been to Goodwood, Ascot, Henley, (and either loved it or thought it was filled with toffee-nosed louts, depending whether she is a whinger or a pusher). Take her dog racing (by which we mean White City and not tying her dog's lead to the fender of your TVR and accelerating from 0-60 in 1.4 seconds)

She will have eaten at all of Terence Conran's restaurants. Any smart place you take her to, she is likely to have been there before and know the people dining on the next table. Go to a good hamburger joint or buy some fish and chips. This will be a complete novelty, and it won't break the bank. She'll think you are surprisingly different. Or else a lemon-livered cheapskate whose wallet hasn't seen the light of day since it was chewing the cud.

How to spot the rival

There are always men around, but these are mostly colleagues rather than rivals. The other suitor is the one with the masochistic, sycophantic look, who laughs at any jokes she might make and constantly refills her glass of champagne. Knock his hand so that he throws his glass of champagne on your intended, and be standing ready with a napkin to dry it off. This will not only cast your opponent in a bad light, it will give you a chance to let your hands wander over her body, and decide whether this is in fact a suitable object for your affections.

Otherwise, get the girl on her own, and ask her if she has the rumour that your rival, er, "putts from the rough" (you know, "goes up the down elevator"). She, being a media girl, will not be shocked, and will of course believe everything she's told, and your rival will find himself somewhat cold shouldered whereas you will become the apple of her eye.

What to give her
Both Pushy and The Whinger would like a column in a national newspaper, please. If you can't quite arrange that, Pushy will settle for a Mulberry handbag, and The Whinger would love peace in Bosnia.

Problem Areas

Pushy will expect you to keep her in the style to which she has been accustomed. Her mother will be a complete drag and in fact resemble one of the more garish drag queens with her livid red lipstick, outsize designer couture and heavy moustache. Let us be quite clear on one point- Pushy loves her mum and admires her, "She's soooooo outrageous" (so's Oliver Reed but that doesn't mean you have to call him at three o'clock in the morning and sob your heart out to him while your partner's trying to get some kip).. On the other hand, until she's 26, she is quite happy to play the field and do whatever comes naturally - or even unnaturally. Her vanity knows no bounds she really would have liked to have been a model, but Mummy made her get a proper job, and she will be in debt all her life. If she thinks she is on to a good thing, she can blackmail you with anything. After all she knows everybody there is to know.

As she ages she will lose any race horse quality and just mature into an old nag.

And The Whinger? Well she's a bit serious, isn't

she? She believed in things, and will not laugh off some slight or insult. You will get used to hearing her favourite words: "That's not funny!" after each one of your gags involving the Irish, homosexuals, Bel Mooney, Social Democracy, Red Routes, the homeless and kd laing. The Whinger is a hard nut to crack, as she protects herself by pretending not to care about many of her feminine traits (body hair, VPL, no make up, her uncanny resemblance to Lily from "The Munsters etc). However this is just a facade. She is necessarily very intelligent - more intelligent than you - and has an accurate and devilishly hurtful tongue when required. She also has a tendency to develop into a self assertive, know-it-all loud mouthed git.

What to say

Pushy and The Whinger need to be approached rather differently. Pushy is as skittish as a racehorse. The Whinger is more likely to be on your case before you thought of it, and you are allowed to be very direct.

To Pushy.

"Do you want to come to the special preview of the

designer sale? I'll pick you up tomorrow at noon, and perhaps we can have a little something together afterwards."

"I believe you explain the rules of polo better than Jilly Cooper."

"My friend and I were just having a bet. You are a natural blonde aren't you?"

"I really liked your article in the Tatler last month. I've always wanted to meet a powerful woman like you."

"Can I get you another glass of champagne?"

To The Whinger

"Can I give you a lift to the march at Trafalgar Square tomorrow? I'll pick you up at 12.00 and perhaps we can have a little something afterwards."

"Tell me how did you get into this particular field of human interest?"

"Have you read Germaine's latest book? I would be fascinated to hear a woman's reaction to it."

(General purpose) "Gosh that's challenging" (As in: "I love you. I've always loved you. I want us to give up our jobs and spend the rest of our lives helping the street-urchins of in the slums of Benares"

Reply. "Gosh that's challenging". Or "You're a fat lazy bastard with no more moral sense than a stoat. You've stolen from my purse, you've screwed my aromatherapist and you've used my Epilady to get the fur off that lasagne you left in my fridge two months ago. I can't think what I ever saw in you. I want you to get out of my house right now and if I never see you again, it will be too soon". Reply: "Gosh that's challenging").

The Office Girl

Under this heading we can include junior secretaries, accounts girls, Girl Fridays (who are always rather better on Saturday, unless your name is Robinson) and of course the ubiquitous Essex Girl. Executive secretaries and personal assistants lie somewhere between media girls and office girls.

When young, the office girl is vivacious and funny. She spends her 7 working hours a day thinking about what she'll spend her next 7 hours doing. She's ambitious, though what for is a bit of a mystery. She does not have real career prospects, but she has enough money to party on. She thinks she's a lot brighter than she is (but then, don't all women?), and she thinks she's a lot more attractive than she is (ditto). Responsibility has not yet taken its grip on her life, but she will be looking for a way out.

Older office girls are set in their ways. They realise it's never going to get any better. They'll always be half in love with their bosses, whether male or female. They will have a mortgage on a flat in the suburbs, and live a life of routine drudgery. They believe that life has been unfair to them, and they could have made something of themselves if they only had had a chance. For three hundred and sixty-four days of the year, they lead lives of quiet, repressed efficiency, typing dictation without a single mistake and ensuring that the internal postal system works like the Schlieffen Plan. On the 365th day, everything changes because that is the day of the office party. For the first half of the evening, she will sit mutely at a table by herself building up a long line of empty glasses in front of her. Then, after the Chairman has delivered his "God bless us, everyone" speech, she will erupt like a volcano spewing drunken recriminations, broken vows of undying love, revealing office secrets that could destabilise entire continents, making vicious lunges at office juniors and challenging the cowering Managing Director to an arm-wrestle. Best thing to do is hit her on the back of the head with a champagne bottle and then fireman's lift her body into the back of the minicab which will take her back to the suburbs and her fifteen cats.

Going back to work office girls are just doing a job to pay for the children's treats, and are marvellously content with their lot, and therefore unspeakably boring.

Where to find them

In any office from, John O'Groats to Lands End. She's the one standing by the photocopier, or doing her nails and talking about sex or lack of sex. She is not very approachable in this environment however - not only is she sober, she is also surrounded by her peers. Better to hang around big restaurants in December and pick her off at her office Christmas party. The office girl will always get drunk - but without the Lucia Di Lammermoor-style spectacular of her older counterpart.

You'll find her in Top Shop or Laura Ashley looking for working clothes during the daytime on a
Saturday and dancing around her handbag later in
the evening.

What music to play

At 16 she'll go for Madonna
At 26 try Wet Wet Wet
At 36 she'll go for the Rolling Stones
At 46 she'll still be listening to the Beatles.
At 56, she'll claim she likes the weird, discon-
nected electronic twanging of Duane Eddie or The
Shadows but this will probably just be a short-
circuit in her hearing aid.

How to spot the rival

The office boy, or the post boy is bound to have his
eye out, so it's worth checking for those first. Mind
you it's unlikely that the post boy will get anywhere.
She's easy pickings for the Board of Directors, so
watch her behaviour carefully. He's exactly what
she's after. If you are not in the position of becoming a member of the Board yourself, you could always start an anonymous smear campaign in Pri-

vate Eye, or drop some unattributable hints to the Times City Diary. He will soon find his position a little rocky, and once he has fallen, she will lose interest.

What to wear.

If you've got a decent butt, jeans are always a good bet. She's working with people in office clothes all day. However, she might think of you as her bit of rough. If you have a well cut suit or a decent blazer, she'll think you are much more important than you are, and might even think you're a good catch. After all, she can't really go much further down the career path, can she? Just don't wear the grey shoes and white Terylene socks or the shell suit. Even she's read that this is the epitome of bad taste.

Where to take her

A drink in the pub round the corner is a good start. She drinks like a fish, but it doesn't take long to get her plastered. Gin and tonic is her normal drink - she probably doesn't like it very much but it looks sophisticated. Otherwise, a decent cocktail bar is ideal. There she can indulge her tastes with Malibu and cherry brandy - and get completely pie-eyed in 45 minutes. Don't let her get on to the Long Island Iced Teas. She'll blame you in the morning, and say that she didn't realise there was any alcohol in it.

Dinner in a Italian restaurant with giant pepper pots, obsequious waiters and Roses for the Lady will work a treat. The waiters will know exactly what you are up to and give you all the support necessary. The office girl will think that it's Ooh so romantic

What to give her

At 16 she'd love some tickets for the rave
At 26 She'll go for tickets to the ballet
At 36 she'd love tickets Young Farmer's Dinner, She can take out her taffeta again
At 46 She'll go for tickets to Come Dancing

Problem areas

How long can you put up with a woman with little or no brain? She may be sweet and rather innocent, but conversation in the morning is not easy. She will follow your lead like a lapping dog, and there is something rather disconcerting about having a discussion on politics where your adversary repeats everything you say. She hasn't a lot of money and if she really thinks you're great she'll hang on to you and you'll never shake her off. She's like malaria or Lady Thatcher, she'll always be around. And when you do tell her, coolly and brutally, that her services are no longer required, she'll burst into tears and ring up her brothers - Garry, Larry, Harry and Barry - to come round and dispense a good duffing up to the "bastard 'oo broke the heart of our little princess".

Good chat-up lines

"When I was flying back form Paris yesterday, I bought a bottle of perfume. I think it will suit you."
"Come and work for me."
"Haven't you seen my face somewhere before?"
"Your wonderful - Let me have a word with my counterpart in Hollywood. I can get you into films."
"My friend and I were having a bet - your hair's naturally that curly isn't it?"

The Bar Girl Or Waitress

She may not be smart but she has charisma. She has

seen it all, done it all and then poured a drink for it. And what's best of all, she can pull a mean pint (ie. a good head). She's working nearly every night, which gives you heaps of time to try out your success elsewhere. She'll be quite physical and she won't be shocked when you are rolling drunk, and nothing you can say will shock her either.

Where to find her

Well that's pretty obvious isn't it? She does tend to go out after work, though, to late nights bars and clubs. Find out where they are and you'll be on to a winner, especially earlier during the week when there's less competition.

What sort of music she likes

When she's out and about, play anything lively, but not classical. It's what keeps her going during her working day (or night). After work she'll need proper chilling out music. Everything But The Girl or even Ella Fitzgerald and Sarah Vaughn.

What to wear

If you chase her in her work place it is worth being

well dressed, but slightly at odds with the rest of the clientele, and being a very generous tipper. In the cocktail bar wear a tie. In the city restaurant wear jeans. In the smart overpriced restaurant wear anything you like. Just don't look the same as the rest of the 40 year old crowd. In the Carlton Club, dress in Andrea Dworkin-type dungarees - we can't guarantee a result but at least you'll be different. Most of all, wear a happy expression. Think of all those dull people she's got to be nice to. You should be the light relief.

How to spot the rival

He's just slightly drunker than you, sitting in her section of the restaurant or bar, making an ass of himself. He's the one you offer to give a slapping - just make the offer, you don't actually have to resort to fisticuffs and if, as usual, the ass is seven foot wide across the shoulders and his face has the strange weather-beaten texture that comes to all squaddies who've spent too long ducking behind bushes in Crossmaglen, make the offer out of his hearing.

Where to take her

Well, she'll know most of the bars/restaurants that are anything like the one she's working in. She'll probably have worked in half of them too. You will find yourself under scrutiny from her people if you try any of those. You'll probably do better to try cooking for her at home, anywhere in China Town or an all night rave. She'll drink you under the table, and she'll eat more than you would believe, so budget accordingly.

What to give her

A large shot of Bison Grass Vodka. Failing that, a foot massage or Pro Plus tablets

Problem areas

You will never know if you are the only one in her life, and it's pretty difficult to check up. She works silly hours so she is unlikely to have cooked you dinner when you come home after a hard day's work.

Her hair and clothes will smell of food, cigarettes and alcohol.

Some people may think these are the sexiest smells in the world, but if you don't you'll find that it'll get to you after a while. Or you could just imagine you're going out with Princess Margaret.

She's used to going to bed at three o'clock at night and not getting until midday, so you won't get breakfast in bed, and you probably won't get what's on the agenda just before that either.

What to say

"Just how did you make that Margarita? It was fabulous. Will you have one too?"
"Sorry - is he bothering you? Do you want me to take him outside and give him a dressing down?"
"I make a fine Bloody Mary myself. You must come and try it one of these days."
"Please may I have some more (do not specify what)"
"Won't you join me?"
"Here is a twenty pound tip."

The model or actress or pop singer

Now there's a fine figure of a woman. She has the perfect body.

She looks great in clothes and out of them. In woman stakes she is the ultimate status symbol. She has a glamorous lifestyle and glamorous friends. She knows where the money is and she is going to get some of it for her. You can even show your friends her photograph in newspapers and magazines.

Actually you do have to be a little circumspect with models and actresses. Do you really want to be the muggins whose girl is involved in porno movies or girlie magazines. She's not just keeping it for you is she? And models are so thin these days that there is nothing to hold on to. You'll be afraid of breaking something. She won't eat anything, and she'll drink even less. She will probably smoke like a chimney - she's got to do something to stop those hunger pangs.

Where to meet her.

Hang out in trendy bars and hip clubs around town. You're bound to bump into one of them some time. Beware of doing this in the middle of Soho, though. Models in Soho are something else entirely.

Failing that you could always become a fashion photographer or a theatrical director and then they'll have to do exactly what they tell you. And we all know it's great to be in power.

What music to play.

Anything very very trendy. Try Nirvana or anything that's recently been released by Prince (the most beautiful girl in the world?)

What to wear.

The first rule is that you must look rich and famous. Either that or you must look deeply trendy and narcissistic, as though you will be rich and famous one day. You want them to think they will be able to relate to you in some way. It is probably a good idea to wear a couple of desperately fashionable labels, and by that we mean anything from Michiko Koshino and Red or Dead to Paul Smith. If you don't have the requisites, borrow some.

Where to take her.

She wants to be seen, because it will further her career, but you still want to be in charge. She probably won't behave very well, because like a spoilt child she will be looking for attention, so don't take her anywhere she will embarrass you (The Savoy, The Reform Club). A quiet restaurant will start her complaining, and besides, she's not going to eat anyway. An all night rave may be what she's after, but you will lose control of her there. Try Annabel's or Tramp. If she's not quite up to that, a reasonably glamorous restaurant will do the trick. Failing that, take her to the nearest pub.

What to give her

A photo session or a record contract would be ideal, but, of course, the likelihood of your being able to do that is not very high. Slimming tablets would be gratefully appreciated, but then she might disappear for good. Clothes, clothes and more clothes is what she wants, preferably with a nice and expensive label. A sunbed would help too.

Problem areas

If she does well she won't get out of bed for less that $10,000.

That must constitute a disproportionate amount of money to pay clothes horse.

She'll also be better known than you, and you will find yourself in the role of chaperone or walker. This will make her head swell, and her opinion of you shrink and she will find another man, which is all the wrong way around.

If she isn't successful you will have an anorexic, wet, misunderstood misery-guts on your hands. She may look great but do you really want to put up with all that angst?

Besides, she survives on lemon tea, and she doesn't smile much because it will give her wrinkles.

Great pick up lines

"Hey, I like the threads"

"You look as though you've been up all night. I won't suggest bacon and eggs. How about a nice lettuce leaf to get you going?"

"You've lost weight."

"I know a great agent."

THE DOMESTIC WOMAN

Well, do you want someone to iron your shirts, mend your clothes or do your laundry? Think about it. You will no longer need a cleaning woman. And she'll get on with your mother.

She'll be quiet and do what she's told.

She will cook well and do the washing up.

You'll have to keep her in constant supply of fairy liquid and marigold gloves, but it seems a small price to pay.

She'll be able to make curtains and will be quite capable of changing a fuse or a light bulb. You might even persuade her to do the decorating. This means that you have loads of time on your hands to go and party (and try your success elsewhere).

Beware! She will have been reading Jackie Collins by the busload between washes and thinks that she can be just as

lamorous as any Hollywood star if she was only given a chance.

Where to find her

The most obvious place to find your little domestic is around the soapsud shelves of the supermarket. She will be comparing prices and sizes so that she buys the one which is the best value.

You'll also find her browsing through the weekly women's magazines in the paper shop, looking at recipes that are low in cholesterol, but high in fibre. You might even find her taking her old clothes to the Oxfam shop or looking wistfully at glorious holidays in the sunshine.

What music to play

Try playing a little Van Morrison. It's unthreatening and reasonably familiar. She'll also feel comfortable with anything she hears on Radio 2, so take your lead from Tony Blackburn.

What to wear

You must look as though you'll treat her well, but also as though you could do with some looking after yourself. She needs the aspect of security, but also needs to feel as though she is useful. Try the old suit or jacket which has been hanging in the back of the wardrobe for months (though if it's got moth holes you're in serious trouble). She is also craving a little excitement. After all it can't be much fun washing the floors and doing the ironing all day can it? You will also probably be safe, therefore, wearing that old trusted Armani.

How to spot a rival

There won't be many of them around because she is either involved with someone at the moment, or too busy cleaning to notice the talent around. You rival, however, will be the one with the bunch of flowers, the charming smile and the good manners. If it is not the mirror image of you, shape up. Or else he'll be Danny Baker knocking at her door offering her two packs of her ordinary powder in return for one pack of Daz Ultra. Take the two packs.

What to give her

She's got all the lemon squeezers and window cleaner she will ever want. A little something that appeals to what she considers her naughty side will go down a storm. Try some La Perla underwear. This will also mean that she'll wear it for you, so you'll reap the benefit as well.

Problem areas

Once you are nice to you she'll follow you around like a Pavlovian reaction. You came You Saw You Conquered and now you can't leave. On the other hand she is immensely loyal.

She is also exactly like her mother, and yours. This means that you will have a triumvirate of women against your every bad move.

Your relationship with her is never going to get any better. She may be sweet, but she is going to stay as she is for centuries, whatever you do.

Where to take her

Treat her to dinner. This will be a novelty - she's so used to cooking at home. Then, if you're lucky, she might invite you round next time. She might embarrass you slightly; after all she's not very used to being looked after, but you needn't spend a fortune on it. She wouldn't appreciate a grand gesture anyway, and besides it would kill all her dreams of glamour.

Good chat up lines

"So what exactly do they do to a herring to turn it in to a floor mop?"

"Tea? Tea? A lady like you deserves Champagne.."

"I've never quite managed to get the hang of Mr Muscle bathroom cleaner. After all, the guy in the ad looks like such a whimp."

The Happily Married Woman

It's always worth looking at a happily married woman. She may have all the attributes that you want in a lover - and few of the expenses. And the happiness she exudes is something rather sexy in itself. She is the playboy's ultimate challenge. Men always think it a little unlikely, but it is surprising how many married women have a little bit on the side.

The first thing you will need is discretion by the lorry load. After all, you don't want to get yourself involved in a messy divorce and neither does she. She will be so discreet that you won't be able to tell whether she's in the market until she said yes. An affair with a happily married woman is glorious.. No commitment. No ties. Just a lot of fun.

The second thing you'll need is a devious and deceitful twisted mind. But all intelligent men have that anyway. Then you must have a bucket load of charm and be a good dresser.

Where to meet a married woman

The ideal is to get her at home really, when her husband isn't there. If there are any children, they aren't your problem. If she's game, she'll take care of them. Becoming a double glazing salesman is naff and being a postman is highly perilous as far as guard dogs are concerned. Try painting and decorating. It's a physically orientated occupation and they all have access to the lady of the house. Her husband is bound to be suspicious if it takes three months to fix her bathroom, so the affair will only be short lived. Perfect for either side. Other recommendations are landscape gardening and window cleaning, which give you the opportunity of visiting more than one premises on a regular basis. However, when the affair comes to an end, you will find yourself out of a job

What music to play

She'll love the music that was doing well when she got married, and she'll probably stick at that age. So find out how long it has been since she tied the knot and play some of that.

What to wear

Dungarees or jeans and a two day growth. You must also develop a bit of a cockney accent. You want your H.M.W. to think of you as her weekly treat, so you must be as different from her husband as possible.

But, though you may be her bit of rough she may draw the line at tobacco stained broken stumps. A full set of capped teeth will give you a dazzling smile.

If, however, your happily married woman's husband is in fact a window cleaner, your success will be surer if you are dressed in a fully tailored suit.

Where to take her

Well it's her house and it really is up to her. Most marks go to the potting shed, though the green house, the kitchen table and the back of the family Volvo can be fun too.

How to spot your rivals

The milkman

What to give her

A ticket to Rome would be nice, but failing that a bunch of meadow flowers will make her remember her single youth

Problem areas

She's in charge. You are on her territory and she is also paying your wages. If you don't perform as well as she hoped, she will dump you like a hot potato. If you kick up a fuss she will say you made advances. On no account are you allowed to fall in love.

Good chat up lines

"Ooh those brownies smell good."
"I've found a truly sexy colour for the bathroom. Do you want to come up and tell me what you think?"
"Sorry, I just walked into the bedroom by mistake. What wonderful perfume..."
"I'll pick a rose from the garden just for you madam. I promise it won't be thorny."

The Unhappily Married Woman

For a beginner who is looking for ways of starting

to be successful with women, the unhappily married woman will do as a practice ground. She needs tender loving care and loads of attention. She needs someone to be nice to her, because her husband is such a pig (and it is always the man's fault, whatever the circumstances). She's ripe for the picking. You must be very careful though. She is also likely to fall in love with you, and the one thing neither of you needs is that. Think about the citing in the impending divorce. It might even affect her alimony, and you mustn't let your little fling cause her hardship for the rest of her life. She may be well be charming and lovely, but there are always two sides to a story, especially a marriage story. She will either be X-ray thin or slightly chubby, depending on her reaction to food at times of stress. Both can be fun. Try them and see which you prefer.

Where to meet her

She's the once crying her eyes out over the nappies in the supermarket. She's sitting waiting for 45 minutes in a bar getting through vast quantities of white wine, waiting for the guy with the beer belly. She'll have a ring on her finger, but will very probably be playing with it. She doesn't really think it belongs there any more. She's very probably sitting opposite her husband in a restaurant silent while he rants and raves about something.

What music to play.

Anything from before she was married. It's been hell since.

How to spot your rivals.

Well, she is still somewhat in love with her husband, so he's your main rival. Do not model yourself on him. She needs something new. You do not actually want to dispose of him. He is still paying her bills, and for the children if they have any. After all, as a novice at success you do not want to take on responsibility. However, you do want to draw her attention away from him. For this you must pretend to be charmed by her. If your approach doesn't work, it's no loss. She's never going to say anything to anyone. Just try harder with the next one.

What to wear

Anything at all. You must blend with your surroundings, and by that we do not mean a tie which matches the carpet. You must not look threatening though. You must look sympathetic, approachable and nice

Where to take her.

Somewhere fun and lively to start with and then somewhere quiet and anonymous to follow up. You are going to have to get her reasonably tanked up to start with, because otherwise you'll never get anywhere. You must not let her feel threatened at all initially or at any other time. She should feel that it is all her decision.

What to give her

A laugh is essential, but you must try not to be the object of it. Otherwise, give her something that makes her feel special but unthreatened. Penhaligon's perfume or a facial would be kind.

Problem areas

She will have major hang-ups about almost everything, from her figure to her wrinkles. It will take her some time to unwind and become relaxed again - after all it has been some time since she had fun.

Can you be bothered to wait? You will hear endless stories about how awful her husband is, but somewhere along the line it was her fault in marrying him in the first place. She will probably be desperately nervous about sex. She's only been doing it with her husband, and that not very much either.

Good chat up lines.

"You could do with another drink."

"What's a nice lady like you doing sitting on your own in a bar like this?"

"Do you want to borrow my handkerchief?"

The Divorced Woman With Children

This one is well worth pursuing. She's got her alimony, she's got her kids. This means that she will have satisfied, at least partly, her maternal instincts and someone else will be paying for their upbringing. You will have little responsibility. OK, you may have to put up with the odd stretch mark, but with the rest that's on offer, who's complaining? She'll be good in bed - I mean she has something to prove, hasn't she? She'll be sassy, probably hard working and pretty sensible.

Where to find her.

At 3.30 she'll be at the gates of the school collecting the kids, if she doesn't work, and they aren't at private school. Look for the one who's reasonably dressed, and looks as though she takes care of herself. She's the one with the reasonable private income. Otherwise look for her in Mothercare and any toy shop from Harrods and Hamley's to Toys R Us, especially around the beginning of term and just before Christmas. The shop that she's in is likely to reflect the size of her wallet. Check the ring finger for signs of rocks, or for a slight indentation where rocks might have been. Otherwise you may end up with a benevolent aunt or a godmother.

School sports days and plays are also great hunting grounds. The divorced mother is seldom there with the divorced father, and her children are distracted by what they are doing. This leaves D M on her own and rather vulnerable to your advances.

What music to play

She might be getting a little fed up with Fur Elise and Postman Pat. A little good rock music is what is required. Try Bruce Springsteen or Eric Clapton.

What to wear.
Anything, as long as it looks as though you will not be a leach on her finances. It might help to look a little incongruous to your chosen situation, because then she will try to put you at your ease.

How to spot your rivals
Divorced woman with children is likely to have plenty of suitors - she's quite a catch. Your rival is the man she's known for years, her childhood sweetheart who has just reappeared to help her through this difficult time, or the plonker walking through the muddy field in a pair of brogues. Recognise yourself? You must just be more helpless and more charming than his. Get that puppy dog expression out and use it for all it's worth.

Where to take her
Arrange for a baby sitter and take her out. Nappies and spilt ketchup can lose its appeal even to a mother. Anything will do. Take her to the cinema or the local theatre.

You could be really creepy and take her out with the kids to Alton Towers or Chessington World of Adventures, but them you'll have to go on those awful rides, and they play hell with your cool, calm and collected image.

And think of those revolting Candy Floss and Toffee Apple things that will no doubt get spread across the back of the car. Worse - the children will expect you to shoot straight because they really want the luminous green fluffy sludge frog you can only get if you hit three in a row.

What to give her

The name of a good childminder if you have one to hand. Toys for the children are always gratefully received as well. She could really do with a holiday, but that seems a little presumptuous on a first date.

Try something completely self indulgent; she doesn't often spend money on herself, or get it spent on her. A really nice hat or a simple but elegant piece of jewellery should do the trick.

Problem areas

As intimated, the children. Kids are amazingly honest and uninhibited. They will either hate you, which is unbearable, or love you, which is worse. If they hate you, your relationship will be short lived. Their affections are more important to their mother than yours. If they love you they will expect you to play games with them, stay with their mother and help them with their homework. They have a habit of walking in at exactly the wrong moment, announcing that they can't sleep or that they have done something really horrid like wet their beds.

Good Chat up lines

"Are those yours? They're really cute." (This is to refer to the kids)

"Your little girl looks as though she could do with an ice cream and her mother looks as though she could do with a drink."

"Toys are so complicated these days aren't they? I only got as far as intergalactic space wars in my day."

"Where the hell are you meant to put the batteries in this thing?"

The Older Woman (or The Woman of a Certain Age)

She is financially secure. Her children are grown up and she has the grandchildren to visit. Her girth has expanded. Except in the States, where you will be faced with social X-rays who can never be too rich or too thin.

She and her husband have paid off the mortgage, and they both suddenly have time and money on their hands. They also begin to admit that they find the other boring. While not perhaps being prepared to dispose of the other half, there is no reason why the older woman should feel she ought to be faithful.

If she has, in fact, got rid of her husband, or if he has done the decent thing and popped his clogs, she will have a great deal of time and emotion to use up. She will just adore the idea of an affair because she is so bored. You will never live up to the memory of her past man, but then what does that really matter?

You will have to treat her well. She has, after all,

been around for a fair length of time, and believes that she deserves a certain amount of respect. She will be probably be a very practical person as well. What is the point, at her time of life, in playing with artifice and creating problems? She will also be surprisingly adventurous in the sack. She's been sleeping far too long with her husband and will be intrigued by things she hasn't tried before, or anything that would have made her mother blush

Where to find her

The county fair is a good place to start. She's may well be a member of the Women's Institute and she'll be in the home produce tent looking at Dundee cakes.

Failing that, she'll be on the committee of any number of charities or balls around town. Give money. Book a party. Offer your services in any way you can and she will be in your debt

What music to play

Bandstand music and a bit of Vera Lynn will be appreciated. If you can't actually stomach that yourself, try popera or pop classics. She'll tell you where she heard it first.

How to spot a rival

He's wearing a sports jacket and has a little twirling moustache. She will probably prefer somebody younger and more virile, and something a little more spontaneous than that charming but none the less doddery old fool. If there is someone like that lurking around, of course, it's you or your mirror image. Just make yourself more available, and be more knowledgeable about petunias.

Where to take her

Tea at the Ritz, dinner at Claridges. She won't understand any of the younger, trendier restaurants around, though, of course, she will do her best. As she gets older, her tastebuds will gradually be dulled, so it's best not to give her something too spicy either. She knows she shouldn't drink too much, but does love a good Gin and Tonic. However, she will be really uncomfortable in a pub. It's just not a place where ladies are seen.

What to give her.

Tickets to the press day of the Chelsea Flower Show; an invitation to one of the Garden Parties; a trip to the Derby. If none of those suit you, and you think she might be offended by a stair lift, how about the soft centres. She, after all, will either have impressive bridge work or impressive false teeth.

Problem areas.

Wrinkles and cellulite, though you must remember never to mention them. She'll be very demanding of your time and any meeting will always be at her convenience rather than yours. She may have a thing about playing with her false teeth, which is a peculiarly unpleasant pastime. She will probably have little clue about modern underwear so you may have to battle your way through girdles and 60 denier run-free support tights. Varicose veins. Nothing is ever as good as it was in her youth. You will be told any number of times that you don't know how lucky you are. You don't know what rationing was like.

Good Chat up lines

"What exactly do they call that hair colour? Spring

Violets?"

"You remind me of Coco Chanel."

"Here let me help you. Then you can get rid of that silly old zimmer frame."

"I'm sure I knew your husband in the old days."

OTHER MEMBERS OF THE FAIRER SEX
The Sportsgirl

She'll appreciate your body. She'll be athletic in bed. She'll be lean and muscled, and totally in condition. She'll also be amazingly competitive and paranoid about losing her skill. Sports, rather like music, take up an unconscionable amount of practice time. If she plays a racquet game, one arm and shoulder will be disproportionately strong, so find out whether she is right or left handed before agreeing to arm wrestle with the other. Watch out. If you lose you are on the scrap heap. As a competitive person she likes to win, and so will be delighted to beat you at her game (and yours), but you have to put up some sort of fight or she'll detest you.

She's strong willed and dedicated and she'll expect you to be the same. She has a weak point, though, it is the fact that her metabolism is so fast that she absorbs alcohol faster, and so can get terribly drunk. We all know that a woman's defences are furthest down when she has drunk the most.

Where to meet her

On the squash court/ baseball court. In the gym. Playing tennis on the next court. These places will give the impression that you both have the same interests. She'll check out your game, so try to work on it. No Catherine Wheeling to try to get her attention.

It's no good walking into the ladies' changing rooms by mistake.
She'll think you're a perv.

By the drinks machine collecting another bottle of outrageously overpriced water.

Probably the best "pick up" place in Britain is at the finish line (or anywhere along the way) of the London Marathon. A word of warning, though. Your sportswoman will not be looking at her best.

What music to play

Anything with too much beat to it will have her starting on her Reebok Step Work Out, so keep it calm and gentle. Do not make the mistake of putting on famous old standard, whether classical or pop. It'll probably have been used in a sports commercial somewhere.

What to wear

Fred Perrys and Nikes are a pretty good start. A sweatband goes down well too. And there is nothing wrong with a decent tan. It makes you look as though you are the outdoor type even if it came out of a bottle.

If you're stomach muscles are good enough, you can always try turning up in your swimming trunks, but remember how bad women can look in bikinis? Man can look that bad too. And yes, women do notice.

If all this sounds far too energetic, you can always

have just been through the shower. Carry your sports bag (which of course you haven't used), and have perfectly groomed wet hair. She'll be dazzled, and will wonder how she managed to miss you earlier.

How to recognise your rival

The one you don't have to worry about is the little whimp following her around the gym, sweating like a pig on the running and weight machines. He might elicit sympathy, but no great passion.

The one you do have to worry about is the tall, good looking athlete who has just beat her at tennis, but turns out to be a basketball coach in his spare time. If he's a basket case as well, you may be alright. If not you are really going to have to work at it. Put some poison in his food. Break the strings in his tennis racket, turn the treadmill on and let it run for 15 minutes before you get on so it looks as though you've done really well. Probably the best, however, is to say you've met his wife. So what if he hasn't got one?

Where to take her.

The club bar tends to be a good start, but you will

be surrounded by your rivals there. It's probably better to get her off the premises. The nice little wine bar up the road will have the desired effect. She'll be pickled in no time. She'll have a voracious appetite, as you would expect from someone who spends all available time exercising, but she'll calorie count too

Problem areas.
She's tougher than you and when push comes to shove, she can outrun you too. There are a lot of attractive men in her world, and do you really want to work that hard on perfecting your body? She'll also be up at the crack of dawn in order to get her early morning physical in. That means that there's not that much time for hanky panky.

What to give her
If you can't manage an even match, a full body massage would be a good start. If you feel that this is a little intimate on first acquaintance, a ticket to Wimbledon finals will be greatly appreciated. Make sure it's the women's final rather than the men's final because the men are far too cute.

What to say.

"I've just burst my squash ball. Have you got one I could borrow?"

"Do you come here often?"

"I just love your back hand. It's powerful yet elegant."

"Fancy a match?"

The Young Girl

She's nubile, pretty, thankfully doesn't suffer from acne and still a virgin. In fact she's under age, so forget it. It's not worth trying for success with a virgin. They'll only think they are offering you their lives, and they'll be lousy in bed. You'll feel guilt ridden and like a cradle-snatcher. Why not take somebody who knows what they're doing and leave young adolescents to pop each other?

She's nubile, pretty, thankfully doesn't suffer from acne and no longer a virgin. If she's over 16 have a party. She isn't that innocent any longer, and she's frightfully opinionated, then she's also malleable, and longing to know more. If she isn't, then you've ended up with a dullard. Look again. She'll also be easily impressed, even though she doesn't show it, and she'll think you're wonderful. An adult treating her like one at last!

What to wear

If you wear a suit and tie, she'll just think you're sleazy. Clubbing clothes are fine for anyone under the age of 22, but after that you shouldn't be seen dead in it. Mutton dressed as lamb or what? Try to look like the sort of man that would be good for her image - i.e. as a bad girl. Wearing a Harley Davidson or a Renault Alpine and a roll of money should do the trick nicely.

What music to play

Listen to the charts, or ask any music store. You'll never have heard of any of it, but she'll be impressed if you get it right.

She will be mortally offended if you get it wrong as well, and even call you terrible names like Dork or Middle Aged.

Where to find her

The school gates will give you the best choice. Once

you've chosen your girl, find out which pub she has managed to get to serve her, and join the clientele.

You could always meet the mother in the supermarket, offer to mend her plumbing and meet her on her home ground. This will intrigue and excite her. After all you are a great deal more entertaining than her homework.

It isn't worth becoming a teacher and getting at her that way. Teachers are lousily paid, and have to go through a very boring teacher training course. Besides, parents take a dim view of children messing with their teachers and you'll probably be had up for sexual harassment.

How to spot the rival

He's the guy mending the cooker, helping her with her algebraic equations, or the captain of the rugby team. The only one you have to worry about is the guy mending the cooker. You're older, smarter and definitely sexier than the others. Letting mother know about him is middling to good. Mother will then ban him from the house, and will be grateful to you until she sees your motives. However, your paragon of virtue is not going to be so happy, and no-one sulks like a schoolgirl sulks. You will get better results if you discredit him to the girl herself. Tell her he's into sadism and you've heard terrible stories about him from his ex-girlfriend. Your young girl may not be pure but she is innocent and she'll fall for that one hook, line and sinker

Where to take her

Well she's still under age for pubs and bars, so you'll have to take her to a restaurant. Besides, this will be something for her to tell her school mates, and anything that's gossip-worthy like that improves your chances of success immediately. What she's used to is hanging around in the cinema and shopping mall.
Her mother might get a little uppity about taking her away for the weekend, but it's always worth a try.

What to give her

Anything that'll make her feel really grownup, but that she can still use when she's a teenager. The

Louis Vuitton sac is not ideal, but a pair of Ray-Ban or Missoni sunglasses is.

Problem areas

You'll have to put up with her showing you off to friends. After all, her gossip needs to be substantiated. Do your best to make this a drive-past though, because kids together talk about the daftest things, and you'll find you go off her pretty quickly.

Young girls have enormous stamina and much less experience than they say they have. They always lie about their age. As a rule of thumb, add two years.

They are apt to fall in love far too easily, and have not yet learnt that it's bad manners to cry when they are given the old heave ho.

What to say

"Let me give you a ride on my hunky machine you look too old for lollipops."
"You must be 21."
"I remember studying that, but I don't think I was

very good at it. I was much more interested in me-chanics/cinematography/ finger licking/painting."
"You should be a model."
"I've got some great looking blotting paper."

The Hippie Chick

This girl was born in the wrong decade. She should have been 18 in 1964, and she believes that if she tries hard enough she'll be able to will her way back there. She goes on a pilgrimage to Glastonbury every summer, and each Summer Solstice she has an argument with the police whilst trying to get to Stonehenge on Salisbury Plain. She knows where Woodstock is, and for your in-formation it isn't near Oxford, and she goes digs Love-Ins. She may not go too much for alcohol, but she hasn't been sober since she can remember (which isn't very long). As long as you're into tie-dying and flowers, man, as long as you've read the Electric Cool Aid Acid test and understand the implications of dropping acid, you'll be onto a good thing. The best point about the whole scene is she believes in Free Love, which gives you licence to show interest in everybody else.

Where to find her

Hanging around weird health shops. She may also have a stall where she sells her ecologically sound (man) hand made dope baskets and pill boxes. She may well be doing a course to know inner self better. She'll definitely be selling vegetarian patties in your local craft market.

What music to play

Any of that weird rock that came out in the sixties and seventies. Opera just is not her thing. A Hindu chant would be good too.

What to wear

Nothing new. Dig out some flares and old Tee-shirts. Jerseys are acceptable if they are baggy and holey. Try wearing long hair and the makings of a beard. Beads and crystals are good too. A moustache is not recommended - they tickle. Do not wear too many muscles, and definitely leave the medallion at home. You must on all accounts not look too healthy.

How to spot your rivals

You see the too-cool-for-his-own-good-man hippie

who's stoned out of his mind? That's him (or is it you). Don't worry about him at all, He's into free love too. The more the merrier.

Where to take her

Somewhere that won't play with her head, man. Try a picnic down by the river, or the summit of a hill where she can be blown away by the aura of peace. Anywhere that has loads of people will have a hippie chick's nerves on edge. Drugs bring on paranoia.

What to give her

Love beads, or one of those silly little things you tie round wrist. It's the only thing that she'll want that's legal.

Problem areas

She'll bear her soul to you and you will find yourself addicted to things you never even dreamt of. There is something seriously scary about a psychedelic trip (man). Magic Mushroom hunting is cold, damp and smelly, and any serious hippie lives in a commune with like-minded people. Can you stand it? She also believes in alternative medicine, and so far there isn't any alternative medicine to stop her getting pregnant.

What to say

"Do you want a toot/drag/tab?"

"Hey this is wild man."

"I'd dig getting to know you better."

"Did you pick that up in India?" (This is to refer to her jewellery rather than some rather nasty disease.)

FOR THE LASTING GOOD IMPRESSION

You've made your move. You've followed the rules. The lady has succumbed to your charms. If you want to keep her or not, you should always have a lasting impression. You do not want to have been a fly by night in her life. The following things you must adhere to at all times, on pain of bad memory.

1   A good haircut
2   Clean teeth and fresh breath
3   A bath or shower every day - and remove any hairs that might be left behind

4	Do not ever leave your jockstrap on her floor
5	The name and number of a good florist
6	Never let her see your little black book
7	Never talk about male hygiene or skid marks
8	Never compare her with anyone else.
9	Always clip your nose hair
10	Always clean your ears

YOUR PERSONAL DIRECTORY OF THE FAIRER SEX

You will want to keep a record of the successes which you achieve, following the pointers outlined by our expert, so keep it here.

Then you will always have your instruction manual with you. This gives sexism a whole new meaning:

Name:..

Telephone number:..

Distinguishing features:......................................

Date:...

Marks out of ten:..

Name:..
Telephone number:...............................
Distinguishing features:.......................
Date:...
Marks out of ten:..................................

Name:..
Telephone number:...............................
Distinguishing features:.......................
Date:...
Marks out of ten:..................................

Name:..
Telephone number:...............................
Distinguishing features..........................
Date:...
Marks out of ten:..................................

Name:..
Telephone number:...............................
Distinguishing features:.......................
Date:...
Marks out of ten:..................................

Name:..
Telephone number:...................................
Distinguishing features:...........................
Date:..
Marks out of ten:...................................

Name:..
Telephone number:...................................
Distinguishing features:...........................
Date:..
Marks out of ten:...................................

Name:..
Telephone number:...................................
Distinguishing features:...........................
Date:..
Marks out of ten:...................................

Name:..
Telephone number:...................................
Distinguishing features:...........................
Date:..
Marks out of ten:...................................

Name:...
Telephone number:...
Distinguishing features:.....................................
Date:...
Marks out of ten:..

Name:...
Telephone number:...
Distinguishing features:.....................................
Date:...
Marks out of ten:..

Name:...
Telephone number:...
Distinguishing features:.....................................
Date:...
Marks out of ten:..

Name:...
Telephone number:...
Distinguishing features:.....................................
Date:...
Marks out of ten:..

Name:...

Telephone number:.....................................

Distinguishing features:.............................

Date:...

Marks out of ten:.......................................

Name:...

Telephone number:.....................................

Distinguishing features:.............................

Date:...

Marks out of ten:.......................................

Name:...

Telephone number:.....................................

Distinguishing features:.............................

Date:...

Marks out of ten:.......................................

Name:...

Telephone number:.....................................

Distinguishing features:.............................

Date:...

Marks out of ten:.......................................

Name:...

Telephone number:..

Distinguishing features:.....................................

Date:...

Marks out of ten:..

Name:...

Telephone number:..

Distinguishing features:.....................................

Date:...

Marks out of ten:..

Name:...

Telephone number:..

Distinguishing features:.....................................

Date:...

Marks out of ten:..

Name:...

Telephone number:..

Distinguishing features:.....................................

Date:...

Marks out of ten:..

Name:...
Telephone number:...
Distinguishing features:...
Date:..
Marks out of ten:..

Name:...
Telephone number:...
Distinguishing features:...
Date:..
Marks out of ten:..

Name:...
Telephone number:...
Distinguishing features:...
Date:..
Marks out of ten:..

Name:...
Telephone number:...
Distinguishing features:...
Date:..
Marks out of ten:..